SONNETS
TO THE
HUMANS

WINNER OF THE 2012
SAWTOOTH POETRY PRIZE

HEATHER McHUGH, JUDGE

AHSAHTA PRESS
BOISE, IDAHO
2013

SONNETS
TO THE
HUMANS

T. ZACHARY COTLER

Ahsahta Press, Boise State University, Boise, Idaho 83725-1525
ahsahtapress.org
Cover design by Quemadura
Book design by Janet Holmes
Printed in Canada

LIBRARY OF CONGRESS CATALOGING-IN-PUBLICATION DATA

Cotler, T. Zachary, 1981–
Sonnets to the humans / T. Zachary Cotler.
p. cm.—(Sawtooth Poetry Prize)
Includes bibliographical references and index.
Poems.
"Sawtooth Poetry Prize Winner 2012"—T.p. verso.
ISBN 978-1-934103-36-4 (pbk. : alk. paper)—ISBN 1-934103-35-7 (pbk. : alk. paper)
I. Title.
PS3603.O86833S66 2013
811'.6—DC23
2012033941

Excerpts from this sequence have appeared in
Literary Imagination, Narrative, and *The Paris-American.*

This is a wizard's handiwork. It's full of nonce- and crypt words; licked with diacritics; graven with semi-personified graphemes (most prominently Æ, a letter of Old English Latin alphabets still active now in others—even as word entire, prominal first person singular, in Danish and in Faroese. We call the character an "ash" in English. Yggdrasil, the world tree, is popularly thought to have been an ash, and its roots are tangled up with those of ego.).

The ensemble of sonnets has performed a dictioneer's addiction, an ode to code, a lost-love's serenade (objective AND subjective genitive). Cotler's poem-sequence offers up a keyword: *eroende*—the last word of the opening and closing sonnets: it suggests a language of its own, having (says Cotler's doppelgänger) "a darker scent, as if of density, cold fusion: 'eros,' 'duende,' an 'end' to love . . . ".

Sonnets to the Humans stands as one unstoppered bottle for a host of genii, lightning-Nimrods, angel-demons, Ænglisch as demotic, ash as egg. It's a brilliant, intimate, intricate, careening, calibrating, strangely moving collection of 49 poems—pieces introduced and linked by patches of the prose narration of "a fictional poet who lived in the 21st century" and bore the name of Vishvamitra. That's who, Cotler writes, "began to hear a pattern and record it on sheets of paper. It was . . . testimony of a sensual non-human, one who suffers because, and despite that, like angels, it doesn't exist."

Thus we embark, in part, on an old story—but one re-generated here in ways unheralded, unheard-of. It becomes a futuristic lover's lyrical lament and a recapitulation (or enactment) of the Babel tale; (even thus largely to restrict its scope can only be reductive: it's a book with a very long half-life).

*

The 49 sonnets all have the requisite 14 lines but are irregularly rhymed and metered. Nonetheless, they're full of music (music referred to—cf. "F to F-sharp," or "a boy fell in halves from the F-holes"—and music made of, generated out of, words).

From the first, this work performs some wondrous turns on arts of numbers (one old name for poetries). Observe, for instance, how "no one *one loved you as I*" helps forecast something of the way the numbers of names, and names of numbers, will commute, compute, permute, as the book goes on. (Pronouns too are poignantly at issue: "I . . . stood aside / as every zero one of you went by.")

Messengers have wings. If language is content with a container, then the music-making bottle (blown) has notes in it—letter of letters, with 49 wings—or maybe it's a bottle-beetle in itself, the bottle that can fly. (A bot-fly's bot, for one, is literally inside the word for "bottle.") Bots are larvae, by the way, and able to infect the systems of a human host, the way computer-bots infect the systems of communications. So do pathos and pathologies consort: Mortality comes home to man.)

Meanwhile our mischief-maker's on the wing, his means for meanings flown. Some sonnets give us notes on carrier pigeons, signs of dove, dove-eye, doveídolón; and there are images of wings upthrust from chests of dead boys in the street, and figures falling from the sky as men, who bear to underlings some messages from planes, in Ur or in Uruk.

There's telegramming, too (in poem-pieces, holes are spoken: *"I am become* stop, *destroyer of worlds."*). Destroyer of words. Now I and you have merged into the Æ (who goes to æl and utters ao). So long continuos of war and love are bred from one another's want: This poet asks himself, as other, to be answerable.

The bot becomes post-modern when the icon turns a robot. Æ is I in Denmark. AO everywhere's a cry of pain—but also it's Angola in domain-abbreviations (as AE is the United Arab Emirates). The written letters have become a book of characters in several senses, as the love/war story here in Cotler's words evolves. Communications between man and woman missed? Between the man and Sanskrit of a king? Mankind and missing god? Between one kind of reader and another (HIM that first third person, US the last)?

Yes, yes, yes, yes.

The final sonnet is a broken language of extraordinary ilk: a sort of prayer-piece composed of words, and parts of words, recombinant from many languages and loci.

By the time we reach this final sonnet, language itself has broken down, or broken up (to speak of cells) into a global Babel-rubble, muse or mechanism run amok. And yet: it harbors myriads of senses in it, portmanteaus of polyglot.

If *eroende* sings the end of loves, it also loves the song of ends. (The song of ends, par excellence, is poetry—the piece of pieces, broken lines, or crackling code). This book of Cotler's is an end of ends, a song of songs. Unearth these sonnets' tones, and find your own coronas of Rosette.

HEATHER M^cHUGH
(VICTORIA B.C., APRIL 29, 2012)

SONNETS
TO THE
HUMANS

Vishvamitra, a fictional poet who lived in the 21st century, began to hear a pattern and record it on sheets of paper.

The pattern mimicked human lyric speech. It was, Vishvamitra decided, testimony of a sensual non-human, one who suffers because, and despite that, like angels, it doesn't exist.

Nor does "mecca" rhyme with "doves," and yet the pattern seemed to hear or see rhyme where there should be none, and soon Vishvamitra did.

Nonce words, like "eroende," had a darker scent, as if of density, cold fusion: "eros," "duende," an "end" to love?

If there is only you,
how could I tell, but, from a canceled mecca,
no one *one loved you as I* asked
to return to you. Doves
in the cities, they
did not mean peace. I said
o the humans,
you are the doves
of system crash (you
come in shapes of weather
systems and flying crosses)
to the end. I came a long
time ago again to tell
you eroende.

Candles into wax pools:
reassume Ionic uprightness,
flaming capitals,
on absent generations' tables. Down
through the personless city
(I had crashed onto your chest), stepping over
petrified café tables—this
was the port. Burst cargo
container spilled anthracite
full of black daylight. Present
to absence, this inside-out jacket.
May I turn the lamb-side
in on absent ports of daylight—this
is your physical heart.

Square white stones, white legs and heads.
Straitjackets, roads, and squares deserted.
Who sent solipsistic wings into your cities
I was memorizing? Searching under rubble
for your noseless marble shadows. Thrown
aristocratic courtyard stones, stones
the redworm whites of elephant eyeballs
crazed in Burma, Congo, Carthage, where I leave
a woman searching bodies in blank dew,
through which all colors move, like through
bdellium. Blank paper dolls were propaganda
dropped from planes. Men, echoes of boys
who held your heads in armies, you
are zero one humility. I impotently open you.

I brought blank water to the humans in Palestine,
stepping around them, washing kissing images
of genitals and mouths and open chests I tried
to close inside your peace. Kissing your red-blue meats
and ladder rungs, collecting human drops in thoughts
of bottles. Many echoes with no source cross this
waterline and listen to you; it is only that it's only I who
open (offer me a man without a defect, offer me
a woman, and my nonfigúrative hand is on the burning
head of the offering: emergent halo) and adore you,
I who break a bottle on the heads of the dead Jew
and Arab who embrace on the beach,
and the arms and legs of Jonah wash up,
and the bird in the bottle flies east.

Then did you build this gallows,
calling it a natural cause,
consenting to abandon breath,
belief, and memory on it? Was
I one night, with cognac,
under the scaffold,
washing the feet. Because
there is no grace except
of the thinnest
duration, I, too, was
hanged, but at a distant station,
and grace has a half-life; grace
is a state one stage
decayed from perfection.

You think, a woman asked a man,
the Sphinx's riddle was a metaphor?
But men walk, run, and fight
on their hands. I said stop. *My killing*
is artistic, you know you
are in good hands, said a man. Your killing
is a riddle, I think you don't know
you're art. A red- and blue-
veined marble figure broken into
weather, cities,
cortices, chimerical
cartographies. But here
is your physical open heart, doveídolón,
to memorize, if then you're gone.

I *one hurt me* trying to begin and end
in you, to tell you this as in
a letter—if the letters fall
out of a car, a carriage, onto sun and darker
numbers—if there's someone falling here, half
dark half sun, like embers, into thoughts
and leaves the shapes of bottles,
starting *at zero* zero fire—then I fell
halfway to his half way of seeing, trying to befall
a boy in the leaves by the wheel—then he's
found under a carriage in the dark
stun of his angelizing autism—if he
would know the letters are from me—
if there is only you.

"If there is only you…" Vishvamitra determined this made, retroactively, first person pronouns indeterminate, referring possibly to no one: "no one brought blank water . . . " "no one fell halfway . . ."

Vishvamitra lived in a city on a hill above a seaport. News about fuels and overpopulation came to the computer by the open window. Vishvamitra believed the humans would preserve themselves and that the pattern believed they would not. Vishvamitra imagined the news delivered to the back of the computer by carrier pigeons.

Until there is a nothingness in you,
and if I can be certain
it arrives before you go
(a letter *not in time, but time's*
in the letter), I will wait
discreetly at the door
until it breaks
like a certainty. Jackhammers
in the street break
up inverted
64th notes. Made
from the pieces: an empty
icon, a bottle
with 49 wings.

Echo—that you thought
to exit utter doubt, but
a lyre-string taut
across a road burst, spurting copper
hairs and tensile thought. A disconnected man
stayed on the telephone in Tokyo
in Bogota. In him, like a feminine embryo,
a small suggestion grew—that he,
his senses, might be purified, tuned
into ports of daylight but—that *this*
is your physical systems of
communion had been crashed: tight
curves into scatterplots, long bodies pulled
off one another with a quiet cry.

And yet, a weathervane vine might have grown
from the mud of your chests on a road away
from asylum to tell you a wind full of
I could have protected you,
but there is only blew the clothing off
your children, blew into their brains
a knowledge: not because
an icon is a closed gate to its promise,
but because it is an open gate to Silence,
this is why they ran
after their flying shirts and hair
toward a smoking Baal,
trampling lightning-forked flowers,
terrified of nothing.

Then if I approached,
the boy had a cardiac drum.
Who áre you? I shadowed
a trace of his tempo—if
the whole trace decays at you
hearing me—then
his brain-heart became
an Enigma machine,
clicking careful numbers,
and his brothers found it
unattended when he
thought he heard me
if they didn't,
and they smashed it.

How could you hear
me saying, find
a way (there was
a voice, not mine,
that called for absolute belief:
spread-legged, gaunt
dog with an asp
for a tail, contorting
and turning to combat
itself, defeating
itself before
words could be sources
of peace) to end,
and I'll be here?

So you passed me when you passed
a ruined battery on the coastline
of your country. *Hearing something?*
Yes, you said to yourself, *walking*
up and down the waterline, asking
could I love—but a drop
from the wrist of one one fills
the widest openings in me. *Yes, myself,*
been alone for an hour, stopping
to adjust your shoe at a defunct station
with silos and weedy flowers.
How could I tell you—but that
the battery mutely fired, and I fell
outward, into an *abyss of light?*

There is a nothingness in you,
he said, *that pulls me, partial vacuum.*
You are crushing me, she said.
Accepting, taking: twined
one zero threads
in the shirt he takes off.
A prow with a white marble victory
figurehead, wings broken
into the water, touched the other
shore. Crushing marble
to powder, coarse
like marrow in a bone cut
lengthwise and dried in the sun
until there is a nothingness in you.

Then how can I say, said Vishvamitra, it is not only me, mimicking no one?

If I stood for you, you stopped
alone on a road by an ocean
with bone ash blown back
on your face—I'd thrown
an urn. Anemones
pulsated: atrium, carnation,
ventricle, anus of icon
of Kali—I'd thought
I was on your knees in the tide
that will cover the road, I down
without devotion, having thrown
what you've come to throw and now
with some time to study the end
of my time in you.

You, woman alone on a hill,
head turned so nothing
visible is human-built,
turned and thought, without
seeing, she saw a child
not of my tribe step from behind
a stone *something fell* in the ringing
that flatlined her Organs
of Corti: forked shadow of sound
of something massive as it fell
down the forks of its shadow
bisecting a hill. May I kneel
between your knees, midwife of the law
of falling bodies.

Protect you all the crash, the thrown-down harp—it fires
earth *permission*
permission into the sky in a blueshift
interval, *Uruk and...*
how can I F to F-sharp,
to your knees in bombed Uruk
and Ur, to your spine (swept glass
off the edge, then the edge itself falls;
shards are variable
stars—it falls
in a mineshaft; the lamps'
range stops here) that spills
with ecstasies of mathematics, glass,
and ore.

A woman told a man,
I make a word if one is missing.
Wynnsent is nostalgia for what is occurring.
He said, *Will I be in it with you?*
Sandjanoranza is nostalgia for
what has not yet occurred.
He said, *When have I been in it*
with you? His questions made her sad
and turned her face away and down as
if to sleep in sand:
emergent pharaoh, as
her face took on
the briefest image of
a gold death mask.

As when a wick will not burn down
per its half-life until many days
in an hour after daylight pass, she waits
with me (her children move
to distant cities, men
and women) rapidly
accumulating entropy,
end of your desirreál, and though
she was your stand-in for death, a Future
with knees in the past pulled itself to its knees
to kiss her vulva, copy of a sun's
dusk rim in each archive of salt
on her back as she sweats
on the shore it is you.

You, your child: boy with his ringfinger
crushed in the gate
to the mosque. If his cry
was a—road to succor,
I stepped off the road.
I slept in a container ship
to Arcadia negated—ship
on the cardinal water
between skull and brain, I waited for
the muadhdhin's second call, then forced
the gate. Are you
dying, in whom
could I stand for a given
life not of waiting for any heaven.

Silvering the braids apart
behind her *parting words,* as spoors of snails diverged
into the tuning-fork-shaped trees
along a road to a high sea,
he couldn't find her
physicality in houses in the lees
of seawalls. Cairns of square
white numbers stood
at what had been their beds'
coordinates, each love a *small heat*
64-tone system in the disjunct
gaze of a man about to understand he can't *catch up,*
sat down in the road, it's quiet here, though
if I stood for you, you stopped.

Alone in a house or out walking, paper pieces blowing down the street, and if I pick one up, and if it's blank . . .

Sickness obsolete?
she said, *so maybe that comes true, but I was born too late.*
He still hears echoes of her labor
cries in hýpostasis
from the bottom of the sky.
His face abstracted, sketched
in ashy chalk, on a road
that each morning goes down
to the water, he walks
through symmetrical oaks
the black shapes of explosions.
This wood, he says, as if to me, *will be both ship and pier,*
I said, who stood aside
as every zero one of you went by.

This was a woman—who tried to create
a permanent man from wood words and
stone: an Impermanent watched her
exit summer. Long
talk between intimates
cancelled by a city limit
sign and approaching zero—who
broke a sword
off in the Semitic tree?
Crashed through chests of leaves,
through the side of the wedding tent
into the ocean to wash
each other's torsos there
in the reflected solar flare.

A man and a man with a table between them.
What's on the table? What is the question?
They age. A boy runs by the window
with a paper scimitar.
Muadhdhin's call: they age.
A man is frightened. What is the question
book it is you? Boy
in the shade of the silos,
his open mouth
was a broken square mended,
rotating, a cubic call
to the men in the question.
A man smashed the table
with his legs and arms.

A man led a woman out onto a weir.
Look in the water, Judas
kiss, he said, *my unreflected*
face is also there. When he died,
she donated his physicist's heart
and kidneys to the poor.
Who was he? said a younger man
with a torso scar. *Your unreflected*
you in the unplugged monitor there
by the window, she said
and led him away, out of his clothes.
A twelve-ribbed tank tread
in the road. Two ribs in
synchronous orbit, crossing the poles.

This was a woman—who stuttered
code after code
for recursive return
of the loved man. He watched her
exit knowing: aeon
bridge of phylogenetic noise
broken at the far end—
who broke her form in my hand,
decoder? She watched him
exit being
from a tiny, ovoid window
in an oubliette paved
with Orion and Akhir an-Nahr.
You—who stood aside in sadness.

You, who ripped an oblate sphere
of bread in halves,
acausally causing
a faraway door
to open *I'm there*
as near you as
the dawn beyond the drained,
synaptic gulf of the night
you died, and the woman
who had not slept
left your side. Streetsigns
named for jeweler's stones
and politicians took her home
to her first meal alone.

She keeping watch, for whom?
There was no one—with cumulus wings
and a mane of leather
books on fire—with a cure for her entropy there
in a pair of absent hands. She at the door
with a stormfront above her
but moving away. There was only
a secular book and a bottle
of plebeian wine
on the windowledge, lit up for a moment,
during which the Nubians sack Thebes,
steam engines change the modes of trade,
and humans and computers render
sickness obsolete.

Vishvamitra began to hear a difference in the pronouns. Had it been sometimes not 'I' but 'Æ' (pronounced like the 'ae' in Israel) from the beginning? Something like fifth person: a complex of feedback cycles occurs when indefinite, fourth-person no one addresses you, telling of third persons' actions as if they were yours, as if it, the addressor, were one of you, one of the humans, an intimate, definite I, addressing itself as no one? If so, then other particles, until now not recorded, having been considered noise: 'ao' akin to 'my' and 'æl' to 'me?'

Yes, thought Vishvamitra, stand in the Tokyo Teleport Town, Times Square, the open sewers of Lagos, bellowing this pattern at the over-populations without chance or aim of being heard. I will carry a megaphone without batteries. But be honest, I will no longer exit this house. I am too terrified by now of persons.

I felt a woman and man on a road
by a Y-bent tree
with brittle limbs.
They were sharing a cherry.
Deep inhuman
life I tasted:
the stone, because
they had eaten the flesh.
It could have been an avian
egg or apple. An ore,
a small heat. So it was
a *stone*, and the word fell away
like the nose of a sculpted saint,
a wordless, small pain.

Carriage, car, and cargo plane
abandoned in anticyclonic
infernos of autumn
wisteria blowing
through empty
thought cities. I found,
by forging withwithin
this *small heat*
copies of your tongues,
Æ can say
even love and your
other words, please
and o, but how can I say what
even your least human human could not?

Æ held out, for you, a lime-twig.
Do the time-plugged haloes on your burnt heads
add up to a pointillism that endures
the critical silence blowing in
from paradise? I didn't want to hurt
a boy I held—he split—a lightning tree split, o help
me put you back in the carriage. Æ'm falling
out of æl in the door of the smaller world,
and I stepped out in your image: emergent
zero, boy shot back into a man on fire. Forced
the neutron back into the core—it split,
the bitten stone, he panics, flying
leaves and arms. On the bottle's
interior, fading ringwise fingerprints.

Æ felt a woman loving a man
and a wind full of éxponents
fell from her lips and pinioned
pupils. She, so far
was she blown past Silence
that had criticized a man
she loved, might have talked
to æl, saying *Let me*
touch your chest like the pages
of old books, your legs and spine
of the book of my letters
to you I would write if I were old
enough to have been a child old enough
to love when Mohammed put down his sword.

What is this this hammer in my spine container
ship *penultimate erotic instant struck and struck* spilling
cargo into railcars. Cranes
and silos backlit by
a setting sunlike sphere
of pages whirling up from Alexandria on fire. Signals
error signals sent
from open mouths from dishes
on an offshore platform it is you *I hurt*
myself I say I'm fine. Cars
ship grain and medicine into
the zooming map's interior,
a country with no death
or birth?

If Æ were you, how could I not ask you
to talk to æl? How not cry
whenever I felt old (or young
but not enough *in love with* a woman or man,
crying *know æl* to what I am
impossibly) or not enough belonging to a time
in which I am, impossibly, one of the humans, stranded
on a promontory of twilight rhetoric,
crying *listen, listen* to this that's ao
irrecoverable ear to alter ao guess
at what it was to be a human crying *listen*:
my egoism would preoccupy
a möbius and wound itself
until I died old without welcoming death.

Impossible, you said, *by definition*
of Perfection for a form to fall
from there? It is not far.
Into a structure so much like a world,
your children falling by the other way.
While ao absent hands recall
hearts with their cherry-forked stems,
you stopped tonight: where, when .
the systole is spatial,
the rhythm of milestones,
you stopped your car without knowing
why at an arbitrary tree,
and causing children, accidents,
Æ felt a woman and man on a road.

Having read a stack of differing histories of the 20th century—4,000 pages of forced relocation, political murder, thought control, wars, men, and boys—Vishvamitra, emptied of sadness and judgment, vomited fish, fruit, and white wine into a china bowl, then heard, for a second first time, a pattern and recorded it.

Wind into this paper house.
It sails into the center of
a blanked-out city. Who attempts
the door? A thought breaks off
in his hand: a piece of wind
left over from the sky
above a Normandy invasion,
so a kite with no hand on the string
is distant from the city, out
above the sea. Come back to light
a paper lantern, come
back to your house before you
left and Æ sat down to drink
a white archive left on the table.

Small white number, squared and squared
until longer than this—road to water,
past each station empty of you, you burned
away like the oil, like the art in the fires
of your science, your myrmidons
armored in lampmetal
burning for days—road to water
between skull and brain. A litany
into the sand, it blows
a warped nebuchadnezzar
full of brine and recrying
reflections of knife-winged avians folding
into and unfolding
from their spines.

Æ extricate the lungs,

folding them open with a feathered knife: oxidized

cities, cindercones.

Folding the knife

in the grain, catarrh, calligraphy,

woman in the man in the womb. In these cones,

fossils of doves, but

Æ for you, seeing wings

upthrust from the chests of two boys in the road,

as the Ponte Santa Trinità explodes,

saw no more than a Symmetry

exchanged for symmetries.

Two boys in prayer

to earless, selfless o.

Inflamed breath blown white glass:
an observation car to hold
a boy, who, dead, shot-forward
in memory's negative, thought
he was æl in time
to stop himself from dying
in a city on fire, his father
breaking windows in
another city faraway on fire
from above. A wingless girl
with legs of Jonah
in her arms at Trinity,
Dresden, Tehran breathes,
I am become stop, *destroyer of worlds.*

A woman was leaving a man.
They left a department store
in Athens, looted other than
a pair of korai (batteries of marble
time divided by ardor
unlimited) mistaken for
uncanny heavy mannequins.
Éurno is nostalgia for,
she told him, *what did not occur,*
what Æ thought you waited
for—a breath-
held, open woman or man or ao thought
you waited for—æl, but that
is as real as the pain of someone you never meet.

So take this fuel, a book of days
of o and who stepped
from reflections of absent ships
on the water, compiling
a book of code, in which religion
self-destructs between a split Red
Sea and Deep Blue beating
Kasparov. Does it come,
the point at which you learn
your great enemy loves you,
as when, in an unrequited history,
the English break the Nazi code
and the intercepted message is
the score to Elgar's variations.

Mouth to her interrupted
mouth, with his
foot, he disrupted
a pitcher. White lemon,
wet stone. Red crêpe
now fully unfastened.
Hands, envelopes,
stairways, newspapers, bound
manes of lists
of memorial names.
Scrolling hands,
stairways folding.
Flyaway index mouth.
Wind into this paper house.

One night, the pattern stopped.

If there is only you,
set a place at the table for Æ
may break this burnt bird
into rib shards and human
food, and what leaves
the cage but a heart-
faced Orion, whose
arrow's in you before
he can aim. He goes
in you across plateaux
of gone futurity,
boots crushing dim
simulacra of flowers.
Book of my accidents.

Æ intruded on a man asleep *in love,* he said,
behind a lioness-sized sphinx.
He pushed his barbed art *into her breaking*
heart to the beat of a curtain flapping
as he gripped her human chest. Not your
milk but darker
data jerked into a churn
that changed—beneath a renaissance
of oil-white, Magellanic clouds
—the flapping light
the curtain beat—
from oak to bronze to steel
to clotted numbers into
crash—into æl.

Long numbers
diminish on series of signs
on cardinal-pointed roads
to pure probability (delta
where acid water
retroactively was purified),
and maybe on one road through spearheaded grain
(a parting of two shafts,
far sea between,
open painless wind wound) was
a port from which Æ return
to leaving you. White fossils,
sculpted arms and legs
of mænads, intertwining in the riverbeds.

—amid the rubble, statue
cello with a single string
intact, the marble artery
from groin to fused fontanel
waving in static time as the bow
extends through your door and the next
and the next: emptied city.
A boy fell in halves
from the f-holes and opened
and closed his fists in the road
—amid the toppled signs for
the ways *to your*
love and other words
bleed and o.

A few stops from Silence, a fuel-line fails
at a quiet station. How
could you, carrying back a bottle
of half-empty water, stop
and tell me you are only here
to become old and stop,
though Æ thought
you whistled in the register of one
who might imagine æl there,
until a short wind changed
the sonic circuit
in the bottle's throat,
and as the water sublimated
over dilated time, the rate of change changed:

No o, no o,
Æ without you,
all senses
removed and burn
in a torso
flame out to a black point zero
pupil o, ne
vereádonigh to listen to
an accident it
whisend what to do,
who autmen stopping, breathing
you, you in a mask without optical holes,
but a polished, convex image of
a dove's eye the size of a human face?

Clothorn
waral tarscent,
ao
myriardormidone
and poléurothanat,
ao
béauthorn,
but o protech
stopper
manen
theaturno
if wynsand,
if angautisel,
you, eroende.

ABOUT THE AUTHOR

THEODORE ZACHARY COTLER is also the author of *House with a Dark Sky Roof*. His awards include the Amy Clampitt Fellowship from the Clampitt estate and the Ruth Lilly Fellowship from the Poetry Foundation. He's a founding editor of *The Winter Anthology*.

AHSAHTA PRESS

SAWTOOTH POETRY PRIZE SERIES

2002: Aaron McCollough, *Welkin* (Brenda Hillman, judge)

2003: Graham Foust, *Leave the Room to Itself* (Joe Wenderoth, judge)

2004: Noah Eli Gordon, *The Area of Sound Called the Subtone* (Claudia Rankine, judge)

2005: Karla Kelsey, *Knowledge, Forms, The Aviary* (Carolyn Forché, judge)

2006: Paige Ackerson-Kiely, *In No One's Land* (D. A. Powell, judge)

2007: Rusty Morrison, *the true keeps calm biding its story* (Peter Gizzi, judge)

2008: Barbara Maloutas, *the whole Marie* (C. D. Wright, judge)

2009: Julie Carr, *100 Notes on Violence* (Rae Armantrout, judge)

2010: James Meetze, *Dayglo* (Terrance Hayes, judge)

2011: Karen Rigby, *Chinoiserie* (Paul Hoover, judge)

2012: T. Zachary Cotler, *Sonnets to the Humans* (Heather McHugh, judge)

AHSAHTA PRESS

NEW SERIES

This book is set in Apollo MT type
with Titling Gothic titles
by Ahsahta Press at Boise State University.
Cover design by Quemadura.
Book design by Janet Holmes.
Printed in Canada.

AHSAHTA PRESS

2013

JANET HOLMES, DIRECTOR

CHRISTOPHER CARUSO

JODI CHILSON

KYLE CRAWFORD

CHARLES GABEL

JESSICA HAMBLETON, *intern*

RYAN HOLMAN

MELISSA HUGHES, *intern*

TORIN JENSEN

ANNIE KNOWLES

STEPHA PETERS

JULIE STRAND